HYMNS
ILLUSTRATED
WITH CHALK

by

Harry Githens

Complete with 29 hymn talks

The Standard Publishing Company
Cincinnati, Ohio
2950

DEDICATION

To

Price Roberts

and

Odella Vonalt

in recognition of the encouragement
they gave me when on the faculty of
the Lake James Christian Assembly
for several seasons.

INTRODUCTION

Manila, white, gray bogus, or colored paper may be used for chalk drawings. Purchase the Manila, gray bogus, and white paper, size 28 in. by 42 in., from a paper company if one is available. The colored paper, called either art, poster, or construction paper, is obtained from school-supply and art stores in size 24 in. by 36 in.

A 28 in. by 42 in. board is recommended. The board must be sturdy. It is best to keep 30 to 35 sheets of paper on the board at all times. The thickness of the paper helps to cut down noise.

You may want to use a frame for your pictures. Suitable materials are velvet, corduroy, or wood. If a frame is used, make a light pencil line on the paper around where the frame will hit the paper. If a frame is not used, make certain to rub chalk to edge of paper.

Use soft chalk, 1 in. by 1 in. by 3 in. The American Crayon Company, Sandusky, Ohio, will send a color wheel showing the shades of chalk available. Have a tray for the chalk built right under the board.

Either blend chalk with hands or with facial tissues. Always blend colors unless instructed otherwise. Dusting the hands with talcum powder before using the chalk will fill pores of fingers and prevent chalk from penetrating too deeply.

Learn to stand beside, not in front of, the easel when drawing. Practice each picture until you are confident of a successful result. Strive for speed with each attempt. Newsprint or the back side of a smooth grade of wall paper may be used for practicing.

After the picture is completed, a spotlight turned on it brings out the picture better. A Rotochrome spot lamp, obtained from display houses, brings out the picture under several different colors of light. If a black light is used, make the high lights of the pictures with florescent chalk.

The easier pictures are in the front of the book and the harder ones in the back. The simpler pictures are best for rapid chalk drawings, which are most appropriate for evangelistic meetings, for example.

Follow On

Where He Leads I'll Follow

HOW TO DRAW THE PICTURE

Paper: Light blue, or cover entire area of white paper with light blue chalk.

Sunset: Using the edge of the chalk, make strokes of light flesh across the paper. Add touches of violet, and blend.

Distant Hills: Draw one violet and one green. Highlight with yellow-green.

Valley: Make yellow-green, leaving open area for stream. Highlight with yellow.

Stream: Add yellow high lights and green reflection.

Foreground Hills: Make dark green with black shadows and yellow high lights.

Trees: Draw trunks with black and make dark green leaves. Highlight with yellow.

SCRIPTURE READING

"And he said unto another, Follow me. But he said, Lord, suffer me first to go and bury my father. Jesus said unto him, Let the dead bury their dead: but go thou and preach the kingdom of God. And another also said, Lord, I will follow thee; but let me first go bid them farewell, which are at home at my house. And Jesus said unto him, No man, having put his hand to the plow, and looking back, is fit for the kingdom of God."—Luke 9: 59-62

"Then said Jesus unto his disciples, If any man will come after me, let him deny himself, and take up his cross, and follow me."—Matthew 16: 24

"If any man serve me, let him follow me; and where I am, there shall also my servant be: if any man serve me, him will my Father honour."—John 12: 26

Sweet Peace

Wonderful Peace

HOW TO DRAW THE PICTURE

Paper: Dark blue, or cover entire area of white paper with dark blue chalk.

Moon Background: Make horizontal strokes of white and yellow and blend together.

Moon: Draw with yellow chalk.

Water: Make with flat side of light blue chalk and do not blend.

Reflection: Make with short horizontal strokes of yellow.

Sky Line: Draw a faint white line.

Beach: Make with flat side of dull flesh chalk.

Trees: Draw width of trunks with edge or flat end of light brown chalk. Make short black strokes along trunk. Highlight right side of tree with yellow. Draw a black line for each branch. Draw strokes of dark green from branches outward for leaves. Make violet shadows for trees.

Grass: Draw narrow strokes of green.

SCRIPTURE READING

"Peace I leave with you, my peace I give unto you: not as the world giveth, give I unto you. Let not your heart be troubled, neither let it be afraid."—John 14: 27

"Therefore being justified by faith, we have peace with God through our Lord Jesus Christ: by whom also we have access by faith into this grace wherein we stand, and rejoice in hope of the glory of God."—Romans 5: 1, 2

"Rejoice in the Lord alway: and again I say, Rejoice. Let your moderation be known unto all men. The Lord is at hand. Be careful for nothing; but in every thing by prayer and supplication with thanksgiving let your requests be made known unto God. And the peace of God, which passeth all understanding, shall keep your hearts and minds through Christ Jesus."—Philippians 4: 4-7

7

Beyond the Sunset

Day Is Dying in the West

Abide With Me

Now the Day Is Over

HOW TO DRAW THE PICTURE

Paper: Yellow, or cover entire area of white paper with yellow chalk.

Sunset: Using edge of chalk, make straight horizontal strokes of different lengths toward you, first of orange and then magenta closer to shore.

Hills: Make violet and green or brown.

Shore Line: Draw a faint white line for distant shore line.

Foreground: Color green; highlight with yellow.

Tree: Draw trunk with edge or flat end of black chalk. Make branches black and leaves green. Highlight with yellow. Make shadow of tree violet.

Sun: Color red-orange.

Reflection: Make yellow.

HYMN STORY
(Beyond the Sunset)

"Beyond the Sunset" was written by Virgil and Blanche Brock while they were guests at the home of Homer Rodeheaver along with other faculty members of the Rodeheaver School of Music. The guest house there is located on the eastern side of Winona Lake and, looking westward across the water, provides a wonderful view of the sunset. As the Brocks watched the rapidly changing shades of the sunset, they were unable to find adequate words to describe the beauty that their eyes beheld. Their thoughts moved to the question of what lies beyond the sunset and what it would be like when their work on earth is done and their experience in heaven is begun. And so the words for the song came to mind, and they were set to music.

9

The Old Rugged Cross

Near the Cross

In the Cross of Christ I Glory

HOW TO DRAW THE PICTURE

Paper: Manila.

Background: First put yellow all over paper. Then for a rainbow sunset effect, begin above meadow with red and blend upward in equal spacing with orange, yellow, green, blue, and violet.

Hills: Make them brown with yellow high lights.

Bushes: Draw black vertical strokes. Make green leaves.

Meadow: Make yellow-green with flat edge of chalk. Dot with red, yellow, or orange for flowers.

Foreground: Make dull flesh shadowed with brown.

Grass: Vertical strokes of green.

Cross: Draw with edge or flat end of brown chalk. Make edges light brown.

HYMN STORY
(The Old Rugged Cross)

(After the first stanza have someone read Mark 15: 20-24; after second stanza, Matthew 10: 38 and Mark 8: 34; and after third stanza, Hebrews 12: 2; 1 Corinthians 1: 18; and Galatians 6: 14.)

The words and music of "The Old Rugged Cross" were written in 1913 by George Bennard. This song has become the most popular song of the Christian faith today. Mr. Bennard first sang the hymn to some friends who were so impressed with it that they immediately offered to pay for having the first copies printed. The song was first sung publicly at a large convention in Chicago soon afterward. It immediately became popular.

> So I'll cherish the old rugged cross,
>   Till my trophies at last I lay down;
> I will cling to the old rugged cross,
>   And exchange it some day for a crown.

Great Is Thy Faithfulness

HOW TO DRAW THE PICTURE

Paper: Light blue, or cover entire area of white paper with light blue chalk.

Sunset: Using edge of chalk, make straight horizontal strokes of different lengths toward you, first of orange, then magenta closer to shore. Blend.

Ocean: Color bright blue with high lights of yellow and waves of white.

Shore Line: Draw faint white line.

Foreground: Make green with flat side of chalk. Highlight with yellow.

Small Trees: Make black.

Large Tree: Draw trunk and branches brown. Highlight with yellow. Draw yellow-green leaves with short circular wrist motion. Highlight with yellow.

Grass: Draw perpendicular strokes of dark green for tall grass.

SCRIPTURE READING

"I will sing of the mercies of the Lord for ever: with my mouth will I make known thy faithfulness to all generations. For I have said, Mercy shall be built up for ever; thy faithfulness shalt thou establish in the very heavens. . . . And the heavens shall praise thy wonders, O Lord: thy faithfulness also in the congregation of the saints. For who in the heaven can be compared unto the Lord? who among the sons of the mighty can be likened unto the Lord? God is greatly to be feared in the assembly of the saints, and to be had in reverence of all them that are about him. O Lord God of hosts, who is a strong Lord like unto thee? or to thy faithfulness round about thee?"—Psalm 89: 1, 2, 5-8

"It is of the Lord's mercies that we are not consumed, because his compassions fail not. They are new every morning: great is thy faithfulness."—Lamentations 3: 22, 23

Send the Light

Speed Away

O Zion, Haste

HOW TO DRAW THE PICTURE

Paper: Yellow, or cover entire area of white paper with yellow chalk.

Sky: Using edge of chalk, make straight horizontal strokes of different lengths toward you, first of orange, and then magenta closer to shore.

Reflection: Reverse colors of sky in water for reflection.

Hills: Draw some hills with violet and some with green or brown chalk; highlight with yellow. Make shadows violet.

Distant Trees: Draw black trunks, green branches, and green reflection.

Shore Line: Draw white line for distant shore line.

Sand: Draw with horizontal strokes of dull flesh chalk.

Trees: Draw width of trunks with edge or flat end of brown chalk. Make short black strokes along trunks. Draw a black line for each branch. Make strokes of dark green from branches outward for leaves. Highlight with yellow-green.

SCRIPTURE READING

"And Jesus came and spake unto them, saying, All power is given unto me in heaven and in earth. Go ye therefore, and teach all nations, baptizing them in the name of the Father, and of the Son, and of the Holy Ghost: teaching them to observe all things whatsoever I have commanded you: and, lo, I am with you alway even unto the end of the world."—Matthew 28: 18-20

"And a vision appeared to Paul in the night; There stood a man of Macedonia, and prayed him, saying, Come over into Macedonia, and help us. And after he had seen the vision, immediately we endeavoured to go into Macedonia, assuredly gathering that the Lord had called us for to preach the gospel unto them."—Acts 16: 9, 10

Blue Galilee

Memories of Galilee

Galilee, Bright Galilee

HOW TO DRAW THE PICTURE

Paper: Light blue, or cover entire area of white paper with light blue chalk.

Sunset: Using edge of chalk, make straight horizontal strokes of different lengths toward you, first of yellow, then magenta toward horizon. Continue reflection in water with colors in reverse order.

Hills: Draw some hills with violet and some with green or brown chalk; highlight with yellow. Make shadows violet.

Shore Line: Draw white line.

Foreground: Draw with flat side of green chalk.

Flowers: Draw heavy green strokes for stems, dab areas with corners of any color of chalk for blossoms.

Tree: Draw width of trunk with edge or flat end of black or brown chalk. Make branches same color. Add yellow high lights. Dark green leaves made with short circular strokes, and highlight with yellow-green.

Boats: Draw with full side of white chalk for sails. Make bottom of boat black and put white around bottom.

HYMN STORY
(Memories of Galilee)

The words of the chorus of this hymn shaped themselves in the mind of Robert Morris while he was sitting over the ruins on the traditional site of Capernaum by the Lake of Gennesaret (Galilee).

Robert Morris, who was born in 1818, was a scholar, and an expert in certain scientific subjects. He was commissioned to Palestine in 1868 on historic and archeological service for the United Order, and he explored the scenes of ancient Jewish and Christian life and events in the Holy Land. As he was a religious man, he followed the Saviour's earthly footsteps with a reverent zeal that left its inspiration with him while he lived. He died in the year 1888, but "Memories of Galilee" secured him a lasting place in memories of many.

In 1874 the author wrote out his hymn and sent it to his musician friend, Horatio R. Palmer, who memorized the words and meditated on them until the tune came to him.

Rock of Ages

The Solid Rock

O Safe to the Rock

HOW TO DRAW THE PICTURE

Paper: Dark blue, or cover entire area of white paper with dark blue chalk.

Sky: Draw yellow rays behind where the cross will be.

Water: Make water at the base of the picture light blue, shadows brown or black, and wave crests white.

Rocks: Outline with brown, shade into light brown, yellow, and white.

Cross: Draw with light orange or dull flesh, shadowed with brown.

Letters: Print with red.

HYMN STORY
(Rock of Ages)

The author, Augustus Montague Toplady, was born in England in 1740. He was converted on a visit to Ireland when he heard an unlearned man preaching in a barn.

Toplady had a strong and energetic mind but a weak body. Soon tuberculosis had seized him. For two years he fought the disease before it got the best of him. During that time he wrote the words to this immortal hymn. It first appeared in a magazine, *Gospel Magazine,* which Toplady edited. He was in the midst of an article in which he was trying to figure out the number of a man's sins when he wrote this poem which gives the only remedy for sin. The original title for the hymn was "A living and dying prayer for the holiest believer in the world." He was only 38 years old when he died in 1778.

SCRIPTURE READING

"In thee, O Lord, do I put my trust; let me never be ashamed: deliver me in thy righteousness. Bow down thine ear to me; deliver me speedily: be thou my strong rock, for an house of defence to save me. For thou art my rock and my fortress; therefore for thy name's sake lead me, and guide me."—Psalm 31: 1-3

God Bless Our Native Land
God Bless America

HOW TO DRAW THE PICTURE

Paper: Yellow, or cover entire area of white paper with yellow chalk.

Sunrise: Make horizontal strokes of light blue and magenta. Blend.

Sun: Draw with magenta.

Hills: Make one of distant hills violet, the other blue, and nearer hill brown. All hills are highlighted with yellow and shadowed with black.

Foreground: Make yellow-green, leaving open area for stream.

Stream: Draw with short back-and-forth strokes of light blue. Add yellow reflection.

Shore Line: Draw short vertical strokes of dark green.

Trees: Draw black trunks and dark green branches. Highlight with yellow-green.

Flowers: Make dabs of bright colors.

POEM
Our Native Land

Lord, while for all mankind we pray,
   Of every clime and coast,
O hear us for our native land,
   The land we love the most.

O guard our shores from every foe;
   With peace our borders bless;
With prosperous times our cities crown,
   Our fields with plenteousness.

Unite us in the sacred love
   Of knowledge, truth, and Thee;
And let our hills and valleys shout
   The songs of liberty.

Lord of the nations, thus to Thee
   Our country we commend;
Be Thou her refuge and her trust,
   Her everlasting Friend.

—John Reynell Wreford

Let Jesus Come Into Your Heart

and

Since Jesus Came Into My Heart

HOW TO DRAW THE PICTURE

Paper: Cut two large hearts of identical size from red paper, or from white paper colored with red chalk. Use one as a frame for a picture of Christ. On top of it tack other heart on which scenery picture will be drawn. Remove scenery picture at the conclusion of the first song.

Sunset: Using the edge of chalk, make straight horizontal strokes first of yellow, and then orange closer to the horizon. Blend.

Ocean: Color light blue. Do not blend.

Foreground: Make dull flesh, with brown shadows.

Tree: Draw width of trunk with edge or flat end of brown chalk. Add yellow high lights and black shadows. Draw a black line for each branch. Make strokes of dark green from branches outward for leaves. Highlight with yellow-green.

Grass: Make strokes of dark green.

TALK

The most wonderful machine in the world is not a diesel engine, nor the motor of a large airplane, nor the engine of an automobile, nor the turbine in a powerhouse; but it is the human heart. The heart maintains life and stimulates the mind; it is the source of human power and the storehouse of human energy. It is a vessel that may be filled with either good or evil actions, and in that respect it is a controlling factor of the mind. In one of Jesus' sermons He said, "Out of the abundance [fullness] of the heart the mouth speaketh."

A missionary was teaching a group of children the beauty of Jesus' life. One child grew more and more intent and finally exclaimed: "I know Him; He lives near us!" The radiance of Jesus was reflected in the man that the child knew.

Peter wrote in 1 Peter 3: 15: "Sanctify the Lord God in your hearts: and be ready always to give an answer to every man that asketh you a reason of the hope that is in you with meekness and fear."

This Is My Father's World

For the Beauty of the Earth

HOW TO DRAW THE PICTURE

Paper: Yellow or light blue, or cover entire area of white paper with yellow or light blue chalk.

Sunset: Using the edge of the chalk, make straight horizontal strokes of orange. Blend.

Distant Hills: Make one violet and one dark green. Highlight with yellow-green.

Meadow: Make yellow-green with flat side of chalk, leaving open area for stream. Highlight with yellow. Add dashes of dark green.

Stream: Draw with short back-and-forth strokes of light blue if yellow paper is used. Add yellow reflections and light brown shadows from trees.

Distant Trees: Make black and dark green.

Birch Trees: Draw trunks and branches with white, adding dashes of light brown. Outline in black. Make leaves yellow-green.

Flowers: Make dabs with corner of bright-colored chalk for flowers.

HYMN STORY
(*This Is My Father's World*)

"This Is My Father's World" was written by a country-loving man, Maltbie D. Babcock. He brings God close to us through the words of this hymn. He enjoyed all of the "wonders" that God has made—the "rocks and trees" and "skies and seas." All of nature spoke to him of God. The singing of the birds, the "morning light," and the flowers all declare the praise of their Maker. He could hear God in the rustling of the grass.

In the third stanza he reminds us that, although there is some wrong in the world, God is still the ruler. When the battle is over, right will triumph, and we can truly say that "This Is My Father's World."

The tune for this hymn is an old English melody of which the composer is not known.

The words for this hymn could well have been inspired by Psalm 24: 1: "The earth is the Lord's, and the fulness thereof; the world, and they that dwell therein."

The Light of the World Is Jesus
He Lives

HOW TO DRAW THE PICTURE

Paper: Dark blue, or cover entire area of white paper with dark blue chalk.

Rays from Cross: Make long, definite strokes of light blue, with traces of yellow in light blue and dark blue.

Water: Draw with flat edge of light blue, and add traces of yellow on both sides.

Hills: Make violet, topped with dark green and highlighted with yellow.

Clouds: Make white with short circular strokes.

Cross and Reflection: Draw with end of yellow chalk.

Grass: Make perpendicular strokes of dark green, highlighted with black.

SCRIPTURE READING

"In the beginning was the Word, and the Word was with God, and the Word was God. The same was in the beginning with God. All things were made by him; and without him was not any thing made that was made. In him was life; and the life was the light of men. And the light shineth in darkness; and the darkness comprehended it not.

"There was a man sent from God, whose name was John. The same came for a witness, to bear witness of the Light, that all men through him might believe. He was not that Light, but was sent to bear witness of that Light. That was the true Light, which lighteth every man that cometh into the world."—John 1: 1-9

"Then spake Jesus again unto them, saying, I am the light of the world: he that followeth me shall not walk in darkness, but shall have the light of life."—John 8: 12

27

America the Beautiful

America

HOW TO DRAW THE PICTURE

Paper: Light blue, or cover entire area of white paper with light blue chalk.

Sky: Using edge of chalk, make straight horizontal strokes first of orange and then magenta. Blend.

Mountain: Make top white, and blend downward into light blue, yellow-green, violet, and green.

Lake: Draw with flat side of blue chalk. Add white reflection from mountain.

Background Land: Make yellow-green.

Small Trees: Make perpendicular strokes of black for trunks. Make branches and reflection dark green.

Shore Line: Draw white line.

Foreground: Make yellow-green with black shadows.

Large Tree: Draw trunk with flat end or edge of brown chalk. Make yellow-green leaves with circular wrist motion. Add yellow high lights to trunk and leaves.

HYMN STORY
(America the Beautiful)

Katharine Lee Bates, the author of "America the Beautiful," was a professor of English at Wellesley College in Massachusetts. During the summer of 1893 she went to Colorado to teach summer school. En route there she visited the World's Fair at Chicago, where she saw the "alabaster city," and further on her way saw the "amber fields." Soon after arriving in Colorado some friends took her to the top of Pike's Peak. As she gazed at the area for hundreds of miles around and saw the "purple mountains," the opening lines of this hymn came to her. A few days later she completed the poem.

Although several tunes have been composed especially for "America the Beautiful," the one most commonly used is "Materna," by Samuel Ward, which was originally composed for another song, "O Mother Dear, Jerusalem."

Sunlight

Sunshine in the Soul

Heavenly Sunlight

HOW TO DRAW THE PICTURE

Paper: Light blue, or cover entire area of white paper with light blue chalk.

Sun: Make it yellow with light magenta rays.

Hills: Color one violet and one green—highlight them with yellow.

Foreground: Make with flat side of green chalk. Highlight with yellow.

House: Draw with short horizontal strokes of brown, highlight with yellow. Outline house with black. Make red chimney and yellow window.

Trees: Draw trunks and branches black, highlighted with yellow. Make shadows violet. Draw green leaves with short circular motion.

Cloud: Draw with circular wrist motion with edge of white chalk.

HYMN STORY
(Sunlight)

J. W. Van De Venter, the author of "Sunlight," was an art teacher until one time while singing in a choir at a revival meeting he felt called to become a soul-winner. He then left his career and entered the evangelistic field. One hot afternoon during a tent meeting in Lock Haven, Pennsylvania, he and W. S. Weeden, the composer of the music, were in their rooms in the hotel when Weeden began to whistle a tune. Van De Venter inquired what it was and Weeden replied that he didn't know. Van De Venter then remarked that it sounded like a tune for a "sunlight" song. He then began to write the verses and Weeden the tune. The next day at the tent meeting they put it on the blackboard and approximately one thousand people sang the song for the first time.

Love's Rainbow

A Rainbow on the Cloud

There's a Rainbow Shining Somewhere

Under God's Rainbow

HOW TO DRAW THE PICTURE

Paper: Light blue, or cover entire area of white paper with light blue chalk.

Sky: Draw streaks of light flesh or yellow, and blend.

Rainbow: Make rainbow beginning from top with red, orange, yellow, green, blue, and violet.

Hills: Make violet and green, and highlight with yellow. Make the shadows violet.

Shore Line: Draw a white line.

Small Trees: Make them black.

Large Trees: Draw black trunk and branches, and dark green needles highlighted with yellow-green.

Foreground: Make dark green with flat side of chalk. Highlight with yellow-green. Make short vertical strokes of dark green for grass.

Flowers: Make dabs of red or yellow for flowers.

TALK

(Read Genesis 9: 12-17.)

Everyone marvels at the beauty of a rainbow. This phenomenon of nature, producing an arc of heavenly colors by the reflection of the sun's rays in drops of rain or mist, has always been awe-inspiring. No one has ever found a pot of gold at the end of the rainbow because its ends cannot be found. Neither can the beginning or the end of God's love be found. It is interesting to note that sunshine and rain must meet before a rainbow can be formed. Sometimes a storm must beat upon us before we can discover the sunshine of God's love. Even when obscured, God's love is there all the time. His goodness is eternal and has no end.

"The days come, saith the Lord, when I will make a new covenant. . . . I will put my laws into their mind, and write them in their hearts."—Hebrews 8: 8, 10

Sunrise Tomorrow

HOW TO DRAW THE PICTURE

Paper: Manila.

Sunrise: Beginning at top, make equal strokes of red, orange, and yellow, and blend downward.

Sun: Make sun orange, with red rays.

Hills: Make violet and dark green or brown, with yellow high lights.

Stream: Make with short back-and-forth strokes of light blue. Add yellow reflection.

Foreground: Draw with flat side of yellow-green chalk. Add yellow high lights.

Bushes: Make dark green, with yellow-green high lights.

Letters: Print with violet.

HYMN STORY

At a minister's conference, a minister about to retire testified that although his long ministry was ending, he was not approaching an end or a sunset of life. He was approaching a sunrise as he waited his call to heaven. William C. Poole, another minister, upon hearing that testimony was inspired to write the poem, "Sunrise Tomorrow."

B. D. Ackley who composed the music to the song was Billy Sunday's pianist during much of Sunday's career.

(Read 1 Corinthians 15: 51-58.)

> When life is over and daylight is past,
> In heaven's harbor my anchor is cast,
> When I see Jesus my Saviour at last,
> Oh, that will be sunrise for me!

35

The Church in the Wildwood

HOW TO DRAW THE PICTURE

Paper: Light blue, or cover entire area of white paper with light blue chalk.

Sky: Color sky behind church light flesh.

Grass: Make green with flat side of chalk. Use short vertical strokes of dark green for grass around trees in foreground.

Trees: Make trees in background with black trunks and green needles.

Road: Draw with short back-and-forth strokes of dull flesh. Make brown tracks in road.

Church: Draw with different shades of brown.

Trees: Draw trunks and branches of trees in foreground with black. Make leaves of one tree yellow, orange, and brown— of the other tree red and green.

HYMN STORY

The church about which this song was written is located near Nashua, Iowa, in the northeastern part of the state. The church has become an attraction for tourists, and it is a favorite place for weddings, with well over one hundred ceremonies every month.

The congregation was formed in 1855 and the present building was completed in 1864. When a railroad came to a nearby town the community where the church building stood began to disintegrate. In 1888 services in the building were discontinued. Although in 1900 a society was organized by a group of neighbors to keep the building repaired, regular services were not resumed until 1914. A full-time minister was hired in 1934 and regular services have been held ever since.

The song was written by one of the organizers of the church, William S. Pitts, who was a music teacher and country doctor. It was first sung in 1864.

Silent Night

O Little Town of Bethlehem

HOW TO DRAW THE PICTURE

Paper: Dark blue, or cover entire area of white paper with dark blue chalk.

Stars: Make with corner of yellow chalk.

Hills: Make with flat side of dark green chalk. Highlight with yellow.

Trees: Draw black trunks and branches and dark green leaves.

City: Make with short horizontal strokes of dull flesh chalk. Outline in black and make black shadows and yellow high lights. Draw short strokes of red-orange with yellow over it for windows.

Sheep: (Outline first, if desired.) Make white outlined with black.

HYMN STORIES
(Silent Night)

Joseph Mohr, a priest, and Franz Gruber, a musician, were talking one day in 1818 on the subject that "a perfect Christmas song had never been written." On Christmas Eve, which was a few days later, Mohr was preparing his Christmas sermon and was suddenly inspired to write the poem from which "Silent Night" has been translated. When Gruber saw the verses, he exclaimed that he had found the right song. Immediately he composed the music (which is still used today) and on that Christmas Day the two of them sang the new song for the first time in their small church in the Austrian Alps. The people of the community were delighted with it, and it was carried over Central Europe by wandering minstrels. It was printed in Germany for the first time twenty years after it was written. It first appeared in America in 1871 in Charles Hutchins' *Sunday-school Hymnal.*

(O Little Town of Bethlehem)

Phillips Brooks wrote the words for this hymn in memory of the Christmas Eve of 1866 which he spent in Bethlehem. The hymn was a Christmas gift to his Sunday school in Philadelphia, Pennsylvania, in 1868. The composer of the music of the hymn, Lewis H. Redner, was then the organist and Sunday-school superintendent of the church where Brooks was the minister. He was inspired to write the tune during the night before it was to be sung by the school on Christmas Sunday of 1868.

Sail On

We're Sailing Home

HOW TO DRAW THE PICTURE

Paper: Light blue, or cover entire area of white paper with light blue chalk.

Sunset: Using the edge of the chalk, make straight horizontal strokes, first of yellow or orange, then magenta nearer the water. Blend.

Water: Make dark blue, with brown or black shadows and white wave crests.

Boat: Draw bottom and ropes with brown or black chalk. Make sails white, shadows dull flesh, people brown, and flag blue.

POEM

Lord! Whom Winds and Seas Obey

Lord! whom winds and seas obey,
Guide us through the wat'ry way;
In the hollow of Thy hand
Hide, and bring us safe to land.

Jesus! let our faithful mind
Rest, on Thee alone reclin'd;
Every anxious thought repress;
Keep our souls in perfect peace.

Keep the souls whom now we leave;
Bid them to each other cleave;
Bid them walk on life's rough sea;
Bid them come by faith to Thee.

Save, till all these tempests end,
All who on Thy love depend;
Waft our happy spirits o'er,
Land us on the heav'nly shore.

—Charles Wesley

The Beautiful Garden of Prayer

In the Garden

HOW TO DRAW THE PICTURE

Paper: Light blue, or cover entire area of white paper with light blue chalk.

Sunrise: Using the edge of chalk, make straight horizontal strokes, first of magenta, then orange, and yellow. Blend.

Hills: Make violet and green or brown. Add yellow high lights.

Grass: Draw with flat side of yellow-green. Add touches of dark green, and highlight with yellow.

Stone Walk: Draw with light flesh and outline in brown.

House: Draw with short horizontal strokes of brown, highlight with yellow. Outline house with black. Make red chimney and yellow window.

Fence and Gate: Draw with white, shadowed with black.

Trees: Draw trunks and branches with brown. Make yellow-green leaves with circular wrist motion.

Bird House: Make house and pole white outlined in black. Make hole black.

Flowers: Draw dark green stems. Make blossoms various colors.

Bench: Make gray with black shadows.

SCRIPTURE READING

"And in the morning, rising up a great while before day, he went out, and departed into a solitary place, and there prayed. And Simon and they that were with him followed after him. And when they had found him, they said unto him, All men seek for thee. And he said unto them, Let us go into the next towns, that I may preach there also: for therefore came I forth."
—Mark 1: 35-38

The Church by the Side of the Road

HOW TO DRAW THE PICTURE

Paper: Light blue, or cover entire area of white paper with light blue chalk.

Sunset: Using the edge of the chalk, make straight horizontal strokes first of yellow, then orange. Blend.

Distant Hill: Make violet with dark green at base. Highlight with yellow.

Foreground: Make yellow-green with flat edge of chalk, leaving open area for road. Highlight with yellow and add touches of dark green.

Road: Draw with short back-and-forth strokes of dull flesh. Make brown tracks.

Church: Draw front with rapid horizontal strokes of white. Make roof gray and steeple white. Outline with black. Make door yellow, windows light blue, and steps gray.

Trees: Make trunks of fir trees black and branches dark green. Draw trunks and branches of other trees brown. Make leaves yellow-green with short circular strokes. Highlight with yellow. Draw bushes with edge of black.

Fence: Make white. Shadow with gray or black.

Flowers: Make dabs of bright colors.

POEM

Country Church

It's just a little country church,
  Not very big or tall,
But it's the place where we meet God,
  And hear Him gently call.

It's just a church beside the road,
  But there is room for God,
And room for all who choose to walk
  The way the saints have trod.

It's just a little country church,
  But we have found God there,
Where friends and neighbors meet with Him,
  And talk to God in prayer.

—Lon Woodrum
—Copyright by Lon Woodrum

When I Get to the End of the Way
The End of the Road
We're on the Homeward Trail
The Last Mile of the Way

HOW TO DRAW THE PICTURE

Paper: Light blue, or cover entire area of white paper with light blue chalk.

Sunset: Using edge of chalk, make straight horizontal strokes of different lengths toward you, first of magenta, and then orange. Blend. Add streaks of yellow.

Hills: Make one hill violet and the other green or brown. Highlight with yellow.

Foreground: Make yellow-green with touches of dark green and light brown. Make tall grass at left of picture dark green.

Path: Draw with short back-and-forth strokes of dull flesh. Blend a little black into path with finger. Edge with short perpendicular strokes of dark green.

Trees: Make trunks and branches of trees at left and in background black and needles dark green. Highlight with yellow-green. Make leaves yellow-green with short circular strokes. Highlight tree with yellow.

SCRIPTURE READING

"The Spirit itself beareth witness with our spirit, that we are the children of God: and if children, then heirs; heirs of God, and joint-heirs with Christ; if so be that we suffer with him, that we may be also glorified together. For I reckon that the sufferings of this present time are not worthy to be compared with the glory which shall be revealed in us. . . . Nay, in all these things we are more than conquerors through him that loved us. For I am persuaded, that neither death, nor life, nor angels, nor principalities, nor powers, nor things present, nor things to come, nor height, nor depth, nor any other creature, shall be able to separate us from the love of God, which is in Christ Jesus our Lord."—Romans 8: 16-18, 37-39

Wonderful Words of Life

Open the Bible and Read It

How Firm a Foundation

What a Wonderful Book Is the Bible

HOW TO DRAW THE PICTURE

Paper: Black, or cover entire area of white paper with black chalk.

Rays: Make center white, first circle yellow, then red-orange, and scarlet.

Candleholder: (Outline ahead of time.) Make light blue.

Candle and Flame: (Outline ahead of time.) Make candle white and flame yellow with red-orange in the middle. Outline with thin black line.

Table Cover: Make top of cover red-orange, leaving open area for Bible. Make lower drape red.

Bible: (Outline ahead of time.) Make pages white, print black, and edges yellow. Outline with thin white line.

POEM

The Anvil—God's Word

Last eve I passed beside a blacksmith's door,
    And heard the anvil ring the vesper chime;
Then looking in, I saw upon the floor
    Old hammers, worn with beating years of time.

"How many anvils have you had," said I,
    "To wear and batter all these hammers so?"
"Just one," said he, and then, with twinkling eye,
    "The anvil wears the hammers out, you know."

And so, thought I, the anvil of God's Word,
    For ages skeptic blows have beat upon;
Yet, though the noise of falling blows are heard,
    The anvil is unharmed—the hammers gone.

—Unknown

Bringing in the Sheaves

The Call for Reapers

HOW TO DRAW THE PICTURE

Paper: Light blue, or cover entire area of white paper with light blue chalk.

Sunrise: Using the edge of the chalk, make straight horizontal strokes, first of magenta and then orange. Blend.

Hills: Make one violet and one dark green. Highlight with yellow.

Trees: Make black trunks and branches and green leaves.

Barn and Silo: Draw with rapid horizontal strokes with flat side of red chalk. Outline in black. Go over roof lightly with yellow. Make brown door and yellow windows. Make yellow high lights and black shadows on buildings.

Shed: Make white with brown door and roof.

Grain Field: Make yellow, with light brown strokes along edge.

Cut Field: Make yellow with flat side of chalk.

Sheaves: Draw with dull flesh. Outline in black. Make shadows light brown.

Fence: Draw with brown. Highlight with yellow.

Foreground: Draw with flat side of yellow-green chalk.

Flowers: Draw heavy strokes of dark green for stems. Dab with corners of any bright color of chalk for blossoms.

Birds: Draw with edge of black or violet chalk.

TALK

By the end of each day every one of us has sown some kind of seed. No one can escape being a sower. When we leave our homes for school or work, when we mingle with others, we begin to sow seeds. What are those seeds? They are words, deeds, looks, prayers, and even jokes. Seeds fall into hearts, and there they blossom either as beautiful flowers or unpleasant weeds. As most of our sowing is done unconsciously, we must be careful of the kinds of seeds we scatter so the resulting sheaves will be good.

Jesus has compared His followers to workers in a harvest. If they have planted good seeds, the harvest will be good. If they have spread the gospel story, there will be a harvest of souls won for His kingdom.

Whiter Than Snow

Though Your Sins Be as Scarlet

HOW TO DRAW THE PICTURE

Paper: Light blue, or cover entire area of white paper with light blue chalk.

Sunset: Using the edge of the chalk, make straight horizontal strokes, first of yellow, then orange and magenta. Blend together.

Snow: Use circular motion with white chalk all over foreground. Make the shadows gray or light blue.

Fence: Draw with black chalk, adding white for snow.

House: Make front with short horizontal strokes of red. Outline house with black. Put white on roof for snow. Make the chimney red, the smoke gray, the window light blue, and the door brown.

Distant Trees: Draw brown trunks, green branches, and top with white for snow.

Large Tree: Draw black trunk and branches, and dark green needles topped with white for snow. Make tree shadow violet.

Bushes: Make black with violet shadows.

SCRIPTURE READING

"Have mercy upon me, O God, according to thy lovingkindness: according unto the multitude of thy tender mercies blot out my transgressions. Wash me throughly from mine iniquity, and cleanse me from my sin. . . . Purge me with hyssop, and I shall be clean: wash me, and I shall be whiter than snow. . . . Hide thy face from my sins, and blot out all mine iniquities. Create in me a clean heart, O God; and renew a right spirit within me."
—Psalm 51: 1, 2, 7, 9, 10

"Come now, and let us reason together, saith the Lord: though your sins be as scarlet, they shall be as white as snow; though they be red like crimson, they shall be as wool."—Isaiah 1: 18

Let the Lower Lights Be Burning

HOW TO DRAW THE PICTURE

Paper: Dark blue, or cover entire area of white paper with dark blue chalk.

Sky: Add streaks of black.

Water: Make light blue with white waves and spray.

Buildings and Tower: Make white with black shadows. Make roofs red and windows light blue.

Lamp and Rays: Draw with yellow. Make details black.

Grass: Make yellow-green, with dark green strokes on edges.

Path: Make with short back-and-forth strokes of dull flesh. Blend a little black into path with finger.

Rocks: Draw with black. Add yellow high lights.

Ship: Outline in white. Make yellow searchlight.

HYMN STORY

Many years ago, as night was approaching on Lake Erie, the pilot of a ship encountered a heavy storm. Feeling deeply his responsibility for the lives of his passengers and crew, he headed for Cleveland, the nearest harbor. Finally he saw the beacon in the tower of the lighthouse, but as he approached he could not see any lower lights on the shore to guide him into the channel. He attempted to enter the harbor, but missed it, and his ship was wrecked upon the protruding rocks. Many lives were lost because of the neglect of the watchman whose duty it was to light the lower lamps.

Philip Paul Bliss, a young evangelistic singer and hymn writer, was inspired by this incident to write the song for which we paint this picture and which has been used for nearly a century. In the song he compares the beacon light to Christ and the lower lights to Christians. So, let your light shine.

Some Golden Daybreak

It Is Morning in My Heart

Some Bright Morning

HOW TO DRAW THE PICTURE

Paper: Yellow, or cover entire area of white paper with yellow chalk.

Sun: Draw with magenta. Make magenta and light flesh strokes across sun. Draw rays from sun of magenta, and go over lightly with yellow.

Hills: Make yellow-green, highlighted with yellow, and violet shadows.

Foreground: Draw with flat side of yellow-green chalk.

Grass: Make dark strokes of green.

Fence: Draw with brown; highlight with yellow.

Tree: Draw trunk and branches with brown. Add yellow high lights and black shadows. Make leaves dark green with short circular strokes and highlight with yellow.

Barn and Silo: Draw with rapid horizontal strokes with flat side of red chalk. Outline barn in black. Go over roof lightly with yellow. Make yellow high lights and black shadows on building.

Birds: Draw with edge of black or violet chalk.

SCRIPTURE READING

"But I would not have you to be ignorant, brethren, concerning them which are asleep, that ye sorrow not, even as others which have no hope. For if we believe that Jesus died and rose again, even so them also which sleep in Jesus will God bring with him. For this we say unto you by the word of the Lord, that we which are alive and remain unto the coming of the Lord shall not prevent them which are asleep. For the Lord himself shall descend from heaven with a shout, with the voice of the archangel, and with the trump of God: and the dead in Christ shall rise first: then we which are alive and remain shall be caught up together with them in the clouds, to meet the Lord in the air: and so shall we ever be with the Lord. Wherefore comfort one another with these words."—1 Thessalonians 4: 13-18

At Calvary

Lead Me to Calvary

HOW TO DRAW THE PICTURE

Paper: Light blue, or cover entire area of white paper with light blue chalk.

Sky: Make dark blue with flat side of chalk. Make broken yellow strokes behind cross.

Hillside: Make with flat side of brown chalk. Highlight with yellow.

Rocks: Draw with black chalk highlighted with yellow.

Path: Draw with short back-and-forth strokes of dull flesh. Blend a little black into path with finger.

Bushes: Draw with corner of black chalk.

Crosses: Draw with brown chalk, and highlight with white.

SCRIPTURE READING

"Surely he hath borne our griefs, and carried our sorrows: yet we did esteem him stricken, smitten of God, and afflicted. But he was wounded for our transgressions, he was bruised for our iniquities: the chastisement of our peace was upon him; and with his stripes we are healed. All we like sheep have gone astray; we have turned every one to his own way; and the Lord hath laid on him the iniquity of us all. He was oppressed, and he was afflicted, yet he opened not his mouth: he is brought as a lamb to the slaughter, and as a sheep before her shearers is dumb, so he openeth not his mouth. He was taken from prison and from judgment: and who shall declare his generation? for he was cut off out of the land of the living: for the transgression of my people was he stricken. And he made his grave with the wicked, and with the rich in his death; because he had done no violence, neither was any deceit in his mouth. Yet it pleased the Lord to bruise him; he hath put him to grief: when thou shalt make his soul an offering for sin, he shall see his seed, he shall prolong his days, and the pleasure of the Lord shall prosper in his hand."
—Isaiah 53: 4-10

Come, Ye Thankful People, Come

HOW TO DRAW THE PICTURE

Paper: Light blue, or cover entire area of white paper with light blue chalk.

Sunset: Draw straight horizontal strokes of different lengths with edge of chalk, first of yellow, and then orange. Blend.

Hills: Make brown with light flesh high lights. Shadow lightly with black.

Road: Draw with short back-and-forth strokes of dull flesh.

Grass: Make with flat side of green chalk.

Field: Make with flat side of yellow chalk.

Fence: Draw with brown chalk; highlight with yellow.

Stalks: Draw with dull flesh and outline with brown.

Trees at left: Draw black trunks and green needles.

Trees by church: Draw brown trunks and branches. Make brown, red-orange, and green circular leaves.

Church: Make front, side, and steeple white; roof black; and windows light blue. Outline in black.

Birds: Draw with edge of black chalk.

SCRIPTURE READING

"O give thanks unto the Lord; for he is good: for his mercy endureth for ever. O give thanks unto the God of gods: for his mercy endureth for ever. O give thanks to the Lord of lords: for his mercy endureth for ever. To him who alone doeth great wonders: for his mercy endureth for ever. To him that by wisdom made the heavens: for his mercy endureth for ever. To him that stretched out the earth above the waters: for his mercy endureth for ever. To him that made great lights: for his mercy endureth for ever: the sun to rule by day: for his mercy endureth for ever: the moon and stars to rule by night: for his mercy endureth for ever. . . . Who giveth food to all flesh: for his mercy endureth for ever. O give thanks unto the God of heaven: for his mercy endureth for ever."—Psalm 136: 1-9, 25, 26

"In every thing give thanks: for this is the will of God in Christ Jesus concerning you."—1 Thessalonians 5: 18

INDEX